SUNDAY EXPRESS & DAILY EXPRESS
CARTOONS

Forty-fifth Series

AN EXPRESS BOOKS PUBLICATION

© 1991 Express Newspapers plc, 245 Blackfriars Road, London, SE1 9UX.
Printed in Great Britain by Grosvenor Press (Portsmouth) Limited, England.
Reproduction by Cloverleaf Communications Limited, Canvey Island, Essex.

UK £2.95

FOREWORD

by

WILLIE
RUSHTON

Cartoonist

I can remember the moment precisely when I decided to be a cartoonist. I think I recall Sir John Gielgud saying how as a lad he saw Dan Leno, or was it Danny La Rue, in 'Puss in Boots' at the Old Alhambra, Oldham and from then on it was to be the back legs of the Pantomime Cat forever. My own moment of truth was the cover of what must have been the first Giles Annual. (1946, I think. Correct me if I'm right.) A simple Tommy with a mug of tea and a wad standing amidst the ruins of Berlin was on the front. On the back, emerging from a cellar, with hands aloft and a white flag, a number of German Generals stood in immaculate uniforms and monocles and Heidelberg scars. From then on all I wanted to be was a Cartoonist. Tell the truth, I wanted to be Giles, but he was doing that already. I know I copied him like a fury – I'm certainly not alone in that. To this day, I still panic about plagiarism every time I draw a baby or a grand-mother. Funnily enough, it's not the notorious Family that turns the eyeballs green with jealousy – it's the backgrounds. I wish I could draw trees half as well. I wish I could use colour like he does. I wish . . . (That's enough wishes. Ed.)

The most important lesson I learned from a lifetime's study of Giles, is that the drawing should make the reader smile, even before he laughs at the caption. That's proper cartooning in my book. And in his book, of course, which this is. You are in the presence, gentle reader, of an Old Master. Enjoy.

Willie Rushton

"Thieving old crow! Her economy runs with a horse cost us twice as much as the petrol increases."

Sunday Express, September 23, 1990

"Private Wilkinson? For you – final demand for Poll Tax from Islington Borough Council."

Sunday Express, September 30, 1990

"I thought a celebration tea with your Uncle Wilheim wouldn't get by without an honourable mention of Kaiser Bill and the Third Reich."

Sunday Express, October 7, 1990

"Of course I know who Lester Piggott is — he's the best midfield player Tottenham ever had."

(Headline: Top Judge asks "Who is Gazza?")

Sunday Express, October 14, 1990

"She's here to get Ted Heath"

Sunday Express, October 21, 1990

"While you've still got some left it's your shout."

Sunday Express, October 28, 1990

"Butch has slipped his lead and gone off to Paris for lunch."

Sunday Express, November 4, 1990

"Latest order from Brussels – carrots are now called 'fruit'."

Sunday Express, November 11, 1990

"Please tell my MP I've got another candidate for him to vote for."

Sunday Express, November 18, 1990

"What this needy family doesn't need is someone to give them Turtle Suits!."

Sunday Express, November 25, 1990

"Your Mum's here doing a Ted Heath – she's come over to take you back."

Sunday Express, December 2, 1990

"Sultanas, raisins, currants, 3 anti-tank missiles, 4 sub-machine guns, cinnamon, peel, brown sugar,
3 Challenger tanks, mixed spice, suet, 2 rocket firing sub-machines, nutmegs...."

Sunday Express, December 9, 1990

"If I'm paying your prices I want one the right way up."

Sunday Express, January 27, 1991

"You and your 'Lets try 'em at their cheap rates'. Looks like another night in cardboard boxes after all."

Sunday Express, February 3, 1991

"The lady next door says can you come and get her Tibby down off our garage roof"

Sunday Express, February 10, 1991

"I hope we've not got the wrong snow"

Sunday Express, February 17, 1991

"We didn't sell you ammunition to waste firing in the air for peace celebrations."

Sunday Express, February 24, 1991

"Now the war is over I assume you have decided to risk the perils of travel and give us a look."

Sunday Express, March 3, 1991

"Take these in to your dad to give me for Mother's Day."

Sunday Express, March 10, 1991

"Stop hollering wrongful arrest – we haven't even found a cell for you yet."

Sunday Express, March 17, 1991

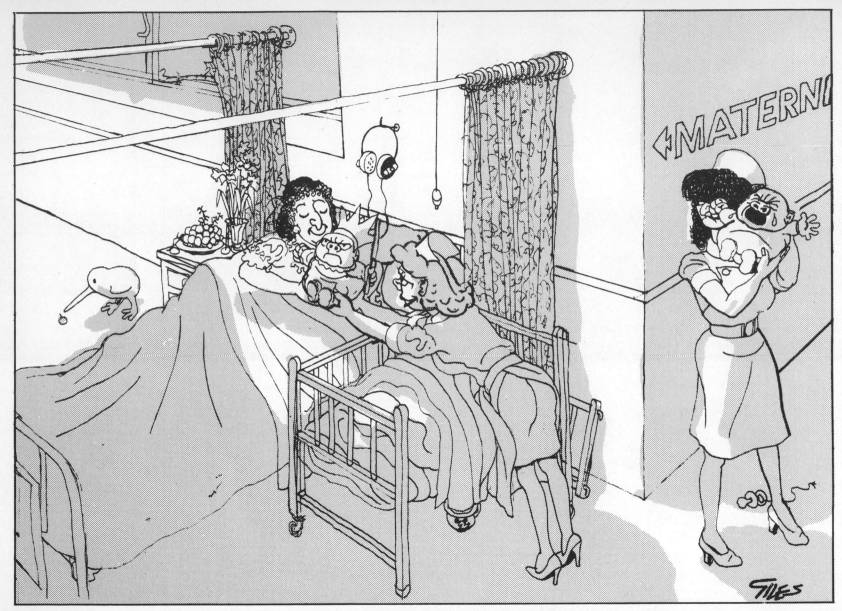

"I don't care if it is one of Capt Mark Phillips's – I'm not calling him Your Majesty."

Sunday Express, March 24, 1991   *(Headline: Capt. Mark Phillips facing paternity claim.)*

"You could just say 'Happy Easter' to them."

Sunday Express, March 31, 1991

"I told you not to trust her with the mower after her horse refused at the first fence."

Sunday Express, April 7, 1991

"I can't say how he compares as a house-guard with the new imported Japanese killer-dog, M'Lady."

Sunday Express, April 14, 1991

"We're changing the route – they'll find out when they get to Land's End"

Sunday Express, April 21, 1991

"Just because you alla come from Tottenham don't entitle you to da free tickets."

Sunday Express, April 28, 1991

"There are some aspects of cricket where they don't object to women joining in."

Sunday Express, May 5, 1991

(Headline: MCC reject membership for women into all-male club.)

"The new juggernaut 60 mph limit also applies to elderly ladies driving in the 20 mph limit, Ma'am."

Sunday Express, May 12, 1991

"Just because our Butch had your Teddy Bear's ear hardly puts him in the pit bull terrier class."

Sunday Express, May 26, 1991

"Do you think his Lordship would mind if we put a match to it?"

"Some people are here who say Grandma has rented the house to them for Wimbledon fortnight."

Sunday Express, June 23, 1991

The following are a

collection of previously

published cartoons

"Never mind about it not being 'arf wot we're giving them – lets git 'ome."

Sunday Express, February 27, 1944

"Taxi!"

Sunday Express, April 23, 1944

"If they keep on bombing Germany, their railways will soon be as bad as ours, won't they, sir?"

Sunday Express, February 4, 1945

"Rare boys for souvenirs, these Americans."

Sunday Express, July 15, 1945

"Be funny if the siren went now, wouldn't it?"

Sunday Express, August 19, 1945

"But honey — where did you get the idea that all Americans live in skyscrapers?"

Sunday Express, February 3, 1946

"What's it worth if I let you stick on?"

Daily Express, April 4, 1946

"Just in case petrol comes off the ration, in future we will assume that possibly the customer may be sometimes right."

Sunday Express, July 14, 1946

"I'm on a bike – what are you on?"

Daily Express, September 10, 1946

"I broke all me Noo Year resolutions first day. Done yours yet, sir?"

Daily Express, January 4, 1947

"Tractors replace horses – de-da, de-da, de-da..."

Daily Express, January 30, 1947

"O.K., here comes one of 'em."

Sunday Express, March 9, 1947

"Well, Madam, if you have definitely decided not to vote for me what am I doing nursing your baby?"

Sunday Express, February 12, 1950

"The politicians wouldn't have said all those nice things about steel workers this week if they had known you used language like that."

Sunday Express, March 12, 1950

"Mum! Cyril's wrote a wicked word."

Daily Express, November 14, 1950

"Determination of the British to have their weddings at Easter."

Daily Express, April 12, 1952

"If you saw Fred's Missus you'd understand him being in love with his tram."

Sunday Express, July 6, 1952

I must go down to the sea again, to the lonely sea and the sky...

Sunday Express, July 20, 1952

"While you're up there, Harry — another one wants sixpenn'orth of best softwood cut off that third plank down with 'no notches'. Repeat 'no notches'."

Sunday Express, November 15, 1953

"All these millions they're spending on education make these pipe racks come out pretty dear Christmas presents."

Daily Express, December 2, 1955

Once again we dedicate our Christmas cartoon to all those spending the holiday in hospital;
safe and sound from the Yuletide hullabaloo going on outside.

Daily Express, December 24, 1955

"Ethel – I'll cycle to work for the duration of the strike without a murmur. But don't keep telling me it'll do me good."

Daily Express, July 23, 1957

"If Grandma's bought a short dress I'm going to leave home."

Daily Express, January 31, 1958

"Madam would go a long way towards improving her public relations with the police if she would kindly remove her car from my foot."

Daily Express, November 20, 1959

"The Express is a bloody awful newspaper," said the Duke. "Ah, well," said Lord B., as they trotted him off to the Tower,
"at least he takes it or he wouldn't know it was a bloody awful newspaper."

Daily Express, March 22, 1962

"Why will people know you only came today because your golf links are frozen? Because you woke up twice during the sermon and shouted 'fore!' That's why."

Sunday Express, January 6, 1963

"I bet Ringo's dad didn't make him practise down the bottom of the garden."

Sunday Express, February 23, 1964

"Git off, you old fool! I was only asking him the time."

Sunday Express, January 3, 1965

"I don't think Henry was wise to say now they've got extra pay he will expect extra service."

Sunday Express, June 13, 1965

"I hope this silly game isn't a stunt to divert my attentions from one of your tricks."

Sunday Express, July 11, 1965

"Best crowd we've had for months, thanks to gas and electricity cuts and my old coke heater."

Sunday Express, January 23, 1966

"He spent all his holiday painting the name on his boat – I hadn't the heart to tell him."

Daily Express, April 12, 1966

"Oi! Before you go..."

Daily Express, August 23, 1966

"Give me the old exotic baked beans and bangers any day."

Daily Express, September 13, 1966

"You didn't plough any fields and scatter – you nicked that marrow from my allotment on the way here."

Sunday Express, October 2, 1966

"Don't get up, dear, it's Mother's Day – I'll go down and make the tea."

Sunday Express, March 5, 1967

"All clear, Ref – the fans have all gone."

Sunday Express, August 20, 1967

"It'll be interesting to see what they do when they come to Tibby."

Sunday Express, January 26, 1969

"Nothing like a Home Office probe into jail conditions to bring out the old flannel in 'em."

Daily Express, March 18, 1969

"She's pinched three of my peas!"

Sunday Express, April 13, 1969

"I appreciate the desire to witness the second half of the World Cup, but I would prefer the choir not to leave at the trot."

Sunday Express, June 21, 1970

"Dad, have a look and see if my tortoise is awake now summer time's started."

Sunday Express, March 19, 1972

"What do you mean you couldn't get to work because of the rail strike? You only live over there!"

Daily Express, March 1, 1973

"We packed the children off to the Safari Park for a bit of peace."

Sunday Express, March 25, 1973

"If YOUR conscience is absolutely clear why are you pouring your coffee in your egg?"

Daily Express, May 24, 1973

"Which is the one you say is a grossly overpaid crow?"

Sunday Express, May 19, 1974

"I hope you'll keep an eye on them, it's the first time they've been to sea."

Sunday Express, May 26, 1974

"What d'you mean 'Everyone will laugh at 'em'. May I ask just who the hell's going to see 'em?"

Daily Express, December 12, 1974

" 'George,' I said, 'Christmas Eve. What better time to ask our new neighbours round for a drink and meet Mummy'."

Daily Express, December 24, 1974

"The calm, unhurried length of time you took to pass me that spanner you should live to be a bleeding 'undred."

Daily Express, January 21, 1975

"Here he come agin – 'How come they're launching Mr. Heath's new boat today when I ordered mine in 1972 and its only half started?'"

Daily Express, May 10, 1975

"Ole! First one down gets the breakfast egg!"

Daily Express, July 22, 1975

"He says his case is urgent. He's been feeling a bit depressed since September 29 1905."

Daily Express, October 20, 1975

"Now this little thing with six sides and a hole in the middle is a NUT, and this little thing is a SPANNER,
but don't worry – it will all come back to you before the Easter holidays."

Daily Express, January 4, 1977

"Right! Thou and me are going to have a little chat about that last fence at the Horse of the Year Show."

Sunday Express, October 9, 1977

"Hear that, everybody? If some of you don't start enjoying yourselves Father won't bring us again next year."

Sunday Express, August 26, 1979

"Did you read about that customer who left a waitress £162,000?"

Sunday Express, October 23, 1983

"I'm getting a bit fed up with you climbing up here just to get your picture in the papers."

Sunday Express, December 11, 1983

"Next – 'Make hole to take two inch waste-pipe'."

Sunday Express, April 7, 1985

"V E Day 1945: "Now it's over, I'll get some leave and repair that gutter and put a couple of boards in that fence."

V E Day 1985

Sunday Express, May 5, 1985

The following are a series of
Christmas Cards designed
for the Sunday Express,
Daily Express and various Charities.

"Right – on the show of hands the turkey gets a reprieve – one of you go to the shop and get six large tins of corn beef."

"Wait till they get to the bit about 'Peace on Earth' then let 'em have it."

GILES

i read a nice little yuletide story in the paper the other day which said the latest atom bom weighs 15 to 20 tuns and consists of 3 main parts.

1. the core, an ordinary little atom-bom as a trigger
2. a thik layer of powder surrounding the core.
3. a thik blanket of uranium 238 metal whatever that is.

when the powder is suddenly heated to an enormous tempreture by the little atom-bom inside it goes off and lets fly a shower of atomic-splitting bullets. these strike the uranium blanket and an atomic blast is produced and highly radio-active atoms are carried into the upper air in the mushroom cloud and fall to earth as death-dust. well i must close now wishing you a merry Xmas and a very jolly new year.

GILES junor

father xmas

Olly

misselto

6 xmas hankerchiefs

nuts

xmas poodings

father xmas falling down a hole

father xmas saying he don't like olly

micky mise

father xmases raindeers with mixymatosis

mushrooms